44 DAYS OF STAYING
HUMBLE

Daily Devotional

Jekela S. Burgess

Published by Mynd Matters Publishing
2690 Cobb Parkway SE
Suite A5 375
Smyrna, GA 30080
www.myndmatterspublishing.com

978-1-957092-93-5 (pbk)

FIRST EDITION

This Book Belongs to:

_____

Date:

_____

*Gifted by: _____

"Make this the last year you struggle, Sis."
-IYKYK (Grandma Dorothy)

#444

To my sister,

Thank you for the humble reminders, almost daily, of how important maintaining the discipline that we work hard to achieve never goes unnoticed and is necessary to obtain. With your balanced composure, your logical approach, and your listening ears, you never hesitate to remind me that

"God's grace is so sufficient."

I needed that.

I listened…I heard you.

A Quick Word

Sis, look at you continuing to show up for and with yourself in this season! As you should because you have done enough for the ungrateful.

Having the same integrity for yourself that you have for everyone else is a special grace that you've had to learn. Amazing job for coming this far. Blessings and honor, they all belong to you. Given that truth, we are back, Lord, with another *thank you*. Another journey to humble ourselves to another level of growth. Mind, body, and soul healing is the goal in this life's journey.

In *44 Days of Staying Humble*, embrace a new journey. One more personal to your Soul Healing. One that connects from the ROOT of our daily triggers to us taking FULL accountability in owning our Response to it. An intentional focus on the book of Proverbs because while studying truths, it was discovered that Proverbs, like many, offers wisdom, knowledge, and a level of discernment that we don't even know we may need.

We will tap into that.

God knows us better than we know ourselves. God cares on a level of capacity that most companionships never reach.

44 Days of Staying Humble reminds us that the Power of Wisdom is not one to take for granted. As we use the direction of the 7 Chakra Healing Methods, culturally, we are reminded that there are teachings, Spiritually, in place to provide the wisdom, knowledge, and power to equip us for our next level of growth.

Every day is New.

Therefore, the chief aim of the book of Proverbs is to bring divine truth into proper focus, enabling us to look at life through God's eyes—from His eternal, all-knowing point of view—and then live accordingly. Proverbs teaches us how to gain wisdom from God's reproofs so that, in the power of the Spirit, we will obey.

Down to the last chapter, Proverbs 31. This is the final chapter of Proverbs in the Hebrew Bible or the Old Testament of the Christian Bible. Verses one through nine present the advice King Lemuel's mother gave to him, about how a just king should reign. The remaining verses detail the attributes of a good wife or an ideal woman. We can all use more advice/wise counsel.

We thank God in advance, for bringing us back together to continue this journey of Peace. For we know, if God is for us, there will never be anyone or anything big or powerful enough to be against us. God is able. He remains King of King, Lord of Lords, there is nothing too big for Him to accomplish.

Faith without work is dead.

Keep going. The journey never stops.

To align one's spiritual with their mental, their mental with their emotional, from their emotional to their physical, the goal is to properly align them all to create a place that is safe, whole, and fulfilling to our purpose in their lives.

We are different in our being, but the more we operate in spaces with like-minded people, we tend to stay the same. Maybe a little wiser, even a bit kinder. When the opposite occurs, where we are involved in spaces with those whose entire being may be a hard, felt, uncomforting space, we adjust to the room. What we call, "match the energy." This is not always the best decision with negative alignment.

The moment we take in energy (feelings, emotions, even acts of others), we are unaware of what this does to our complete aura. To breakdown the cause and effect of our own emotional transitions, according to our bodies, the relation to the 7 Chakra Healing methods, used in this series allows us to define each level of personal trigger to lead to self-development. Chakras can be thought of as portals through which energy is exchanged between the physical body and the universe. Bridging the gap between physical and spiritual, understanding the 7 chakras can help with healing and growth.

44 Days of Being Humble started with a SAFE place. The root chakra's intention is the balance point between above and below, and a blockage can make all aspects of life feel unbalanced and/or unsafe. It's known to be in the base of our spine. The color representation is red. The mantra: I AM.

Who doesn't want to feel safe?

In *44 Days of Staying Humble*, we transition to the Sacral Chakra. The representation of creativity, life, passion, and desire. The color is Orange. This is felt in your lower abdomen. The mantra: I FEEL.

As we journey together, learning discipline along with vulnerability is not going to be an easy task. It's not supposed to be.

Give thanks and remain humble.

Pray for more wisdom, in His healing and, more importantly, in His teaching.

FOOD FOR THOUGHT
#soulFOOD

"Creativity is seeing what others see and thinking what no one else ever thought."

— Albert Einstein

"Don't wait for inspiration. It comes while working."

— Henri Matisse

"There is no doubt that creativity is the most important human resource of all. Without creativity, there would be no progress, and we would be forever repeating the same patterns."

— Edward De Bono

"Create with the heart; build with the mind."

— Criss Jami

"You can't use up creativity. The more you use, the more you have."

— Maya Angelou

"Everything you can imagine is real."

— Pablo Picasso

"Odd how the creative power at once brings the whole universe to order."

— Virginia Woolf

"The worst enemy to creativity is self-doubt."

— Sylvia Plath

"Make visible what, without you, might perhaps never have been seen."

— Oprah Winfrey

Just for Me

"Keep on making a way, making a way... JUST FOR ME"
- Kirk Franklin (Just for Me)

Proverbs 11:30 reminds us, "What does it mean that he who wins souls is wise." A similar passage is found in Daniel 12:3, "Those who are wise will shine as bright as the sky, and those who lead many to righteousness will shine like the stars forever" (NLT).

In *44 Days of Being Humble*, we grasp the understanding of what it takes for one to create their own discipline to maintain their daily mindfulness.

So why wouldn't we want to shine like the stars forever?

When we realize that being humble and staying humble are two separate acts of grace, we will be cautious to take two separate approaches. We will be cautious in our words and our actions, and our time spent becomes a primary focus.

What gets you there, may not KEEP you there.

Is the humble lesson that should be taken from the separating of the acts of grace to Stay humble, it gets better?

Remember to Soul Search.

In the search of your soul, you will find yourself often detaching from your ego. It's a detachment that we often don't know that we need.

In *44 Days of Being Humble*, we separate one's ego from their soul.

For what shall it profit a man, if he shall gain the whole world, and lose his own soul? Mark 8:34-38.

Be humble. Stay humble.

…it gets better.

It Always Gets

"Friends will leave you all by yourself
But don't cry."
- Le'Andria Johnson (Better Days)

You're doing better than good and better than most.

Remember, we all will face challenges that we must learn to deal with, accept, or even adjust from. When things happen to you, they can make you bitter, or they can make you better. Control your emotions. Most things are still not happening *to* you, they are happening *for* you.

Proverbs 29:11 reminds us, "A fool expresses all his emotions, but a wise person controls them." You have the control to realign your thinking. Thinking first to allow the space for accountability to take place. When accountability is present, the healing becomes personal. Take it there.

How much time do you spend building yourself? Working on you, for you? In comparison to how much time you spend indulging in the lifestyles, entertainment, and even growth of others—most you don't even really know? How much time you've truly invested?

If your expectations are of your days getting better, day by day, your goal should be working on yourself moment by moment. Learning yourself, observing yourself, then adjusting to healing yourself to the capacity of your own hurt or inflictions.

Allowing yourself enough grace to discern and accept that what God has for you, it will forever be for you. That will be key.

His will is not your will. Therefore, His plans are not your plan.

Stay humble and always prepared to face the reality of reality. It is well.

Stay humble, give thanks (for it all).

Unspeakable Joy

"Joy, Joy, down in my soul.
Sweet beautiful, soul-saving Joy. "
- The Georgia Mass Choir/ Kirk Franklin

Proverbs 17:22 reminds us, A joyful heart is good medicine, but a crushed spirit dries up the bones." Refuse to let the work of the enemy destroy/crush anything you possess. How do you do this? You remind yourself that the joy you have, they did not give it to you, therefore, they cannot take it away. We have all heard this colloquialism before, but how often do we apply it?

Knowing this, we realize that staying humble truly requires more work and effort than being humble. In this process, growth becomes both inevitable and uncomfortable, knowing that staying humble is generally a response to inflicted pain, caused by others. Being humble is a refined discipline required to avoid prideful or harmful ways.

We train our minds to think past our situations to reach a level of growth where our sides of the story never have to be told. Stay humble.

Learning that the best and most common practice will center back to the focus and the healing of you, requiring you to align your focus differently. Allowing yourself to recognize your triggers will immediately cause your way of thinking to produce a humble response versus the act/art of matching someone else's hurt feelings. It's not necessary.

Reciprocity, however, is defined as the practice of exchanging things with others for mutual benefit, especially privileges granted by one country or organization to another.

Understanding the pure difference of "matching someone's energy" vs. the art of reciprocity will keep you humble.

Adversity introduces one to themselves.

Evaluate where you are.

Give thanks.

Remain Humble.

Endow Me

"To lay hands, and to discern.
To understand God's holy word"
- Coko ft. Faith Evans, Fantasia, and Lil Mo

Proverbs 8:21 reminds us, "I give riches to those who love me, and I fill their houses with treasures."

Lord, we thank you for your exchange of love. Your love is present, fulfilling. Your love is RICH.

Gaining the understanding of how to physically transition out of your "hard seasons," the richness in the content becomes one less of financial need but for the richness of a higher power. This is defined, exchanged as your new definition of wealth, spiritual wealth, and cultivation of oneself. In addition to being rich in spirit, having an endowed emotional strength that we can't explain, will keep us humble in the seasons of transitions.

Change is good. Being rich in spirit is even better.

Remember to not focus on what you don't have but to remind yourself daily that "you have not because you ask not." If you have it, ask yourself how far your current discipline will take you to reach the richness that you alone deserve. Staying humble requires this.

It's an added discipline that we, in most cases, don't know we need. In any place of transition, making wise decisions is often taught, Radical decisions are most often made. Reminding us that no matter the expected outcome, there will always be a plan for your purpose. It is still your responsibility to discover your own purpose. Never allow yourself to be stuck. If you get stuck, never stay there.

God is able.

God is RICH.

PASS ME NOT

"Pass me not ole gentle Savior, Hear my humble cry."
- Pastor Dewey Smith

Proverbs 3:1-4 - My son, forget not my law; but let your heart keep my commandments: For length of days, and long life, and peace, shall they add to you. Let not mercy and truth forsake you: bind them about your neck; write them upon the table of your heart: So, shall you find favor and good understanding in the sight of God and man.

How important is it for us to find favor in others? Also knowing that favor had not always been on your side.

Or was it?

Proverbs 3:3-8 is one of my favorite, most humble reminders. "Don't ever let love and loyalty leave you. Tie them around your neck and write them on your heart. Then God will be pleased and think well of you and so will everyone else."

Trust the Lord completely, and don't depend on your own knowledge. With every step you take, think about what He wants, and He will help you go the right way. Don't trust in your own wisdom, but fear and respect the Lord and stay away from evil. If you do this, it will be like a refreshing drink and medicine for your body."

The blessings of wisdom, Lord, we thank you.

Psychologists tend to agree that wisdom involves an integration of knowledge, experience, and deep understanding, as well as a tolerance for the uncertainties of life. There's an awareness of how things play out over time, and it confers a sense of balance. Having a daily balance of trusted humility is what brings ultimate peace. Trusted, because I know that HIS will is forever greater than my own.

Having the wisdom to navigate through the decisions of the day.

Having the peace to maintain it all.

God is great. It is that simple.

"Let me at thy throne of mercy, find a sweet relief."

Have balance.

Stay humble.

Father Know Best

"See a parent fails, if the child never learns how to fly"
- Kirk Franklin

Having wisdom and understanding what is happening in your life requires more than wisdom. Your Father knows best.

"So, whatever you see, keep working on me."

God's comfort is something we require. Another necessity we may not know or understand why we need it...but GOD! In life, we will make mistakes, we're supposed to. To have someone who comforts you and always understands your ways, during wrong-doing, repeated cycles, and even gigantic disasters is a blessing. God, you are always there. Your guidance is my truth.

Proverbs 16:3 reminds us, "Commit to the Lord whatever you do, and he will establish your plans." However, if we keep reading, we will also see that Proverbs 16:9 tells us that "we can make our plans, but the Lord determines our steps."

We thank you for your word, your wisdom, your healing, and your comfort. We also are humble enough to thank you for not knowing. Thank you for the space we create to allow ourselves the wisdom we need to grow. It is nothing compared to the grace you give us to figure it out.

In His daily practice of discipline, we find all sorts of promises we take to heart and try to keep in mind. We learn that God cares for us and will not leave us or forsake us and that His grace is sufficient. He loves those who belong to Him, and has compassion on us.

It's His comfort and peace for me.

In our suffering, we receive comfort from God when we draw near to Him. And we draw near to God through prayer, reading biblical references to maintain our own understanding, and meditating on scripture.

We thank you for being a vessel of comfort. Please continue to hold me close, and don't let me go.

Staying humble is the goal. Being humble is the key.

SMILE

"Today's a new day, but there is no sunshine."
- Kirk Franklin

Being in good spirits when everything feels weighted doesn't always feel like you're in a good spirit. In most cases, we smile anyway. We push our way through. Growing through life and going through life are like the exchange of being humble versus staying humble. Two separate acts of grace. What exactly are acts of grace?

God's grace is usually defined as undeserved favor.

Who measures what we deserve and what we don't deserve?

Grace cannot be earned. It is something that is freely given. We count on God's grace and the bridge he built in our relationship with him. Bible verses about grace abound.

Proverbs 11:16-20 reminds us, "A kindhearted woman gains honor, but ruthless men gain only wealth. Those who are kind benefit themselves, but the cruel bring ruin on themselves. A wicked person earns deceptive wages, but the one who sows righteousness reaps a sure reward. Truly the righteous attain life, but whoever pursues evil finds death. The Lord detests those whose hearts are perverse, but he delights in those whose ways are blameless."

Remember, there's a BIG GOD, that sits high and looks low. There is no need to go through life trying to figure things out. The peace He gives us in reminding us to lean not on our own understanding are whispers of love. The reminders of pockets of peace assure us it is already done. Because it *is* already done, choose to remain in positions where you have room enough to receive the good with the bad. Life happens, but it gets better. Give thanks for the favor that He provides. "Favor is never fair," but neither is life.

God remains Faithful.

Remain humble. Smile.

It's already done.

Day 8

I'm free

"God will Show up and Show Out."
- John P Kee

Every single time and in EVERY single way. God can do ALL things but FAIL.

If you haven't noticed by now, the reference in this reading centers primarily around the book of Proverbs. In my studies, I learned that this one book had the answers to a lot of the et cetera or dot, dot, dots, which are the thoughts usually left in my head after hearing or reading a passage of understanding. Becoming reliant on the teaching that Proverbs had alone, I wanted to focus in on a higher and deeper level of growth/spiritual overflow.

Much of the book of Proverbs should be understood as principles for living rather than promises for life. In the first seven verses of Solomon's introduction to the book, he indicated that these were guidelines to obtain understanding, but true wisdom comes from the Lord. Think of Proverbs as a tool—a gateway, to a clearer understanding.

Proverbs tells us that wisdom and understanding are more valuable than silver, gold, and fine jewels. It also says that nothing you could possibly want can compare to acquiring them. Wisdom and understanding go hand-in-hand with long life, riches, honor, pleasantness, and peace. They are a tree of life to those who lay hold of them, and those who hold fast to wisdom and understanding will be blessed.

Proverbs 4:5-9 reminds us, to "try to get wisdom and understanding. Don't forget my teaching or ignore what I say. Don't turn away from wisdom, and she will protect you. Love her, and she will keep you safe. The first step to becoming wise is to look for wisdom, so use everything you must to get understanding. Love wisdom, and she will make you great. Hold on to wisdom, and she will bring you honor. Wisdom will reward you with a crown of honor and glory."

Wisdom is not only something we gain with experience. Wisdom is putting our understanding to use.

WHAT IS THIS

"Whatever it is, it won't let me."
- D. Lemon

What is this?

Have you ever felt a shift that you could not explain? Not even a little bit.

A cosmic shift, a magnetitic force, an unexpected separation or urge to separate.

Have you ever known there was a change of some sort but didn't know what caused it? Some people would say it was "the devil." Others will say, it was God, not knowing the reality. It was you. In every situation we face, we should not be so quick to force blame on the opposite of our offense. Being in a position to take accountability, whole heart actually includes one's whole heart.

Proverbs 4:23 reminds us, above all else, to guard our heart, for it is the wellspring of life. A wellspring means a bountiful source of something. God owns everything. Therefore, we truly have nothing. Stay humble, give thanks. Even in the Song of David, we are reminded that the earth and everything in it belong to the Lord. The world and all its people belong to Him. He built the earth on the water. He built it over the rivers. Psalm 24:1-2.

In this study, I wanted to not only know the meaning of account-ability, I wanted to know the principles. I wanted to understand the deeper meaning of the reaping versus the sowing. Not one pain, in-fliction, or hurt could change this. I needed more wisdom. In my studies, I soon learned there were five principles of accountability based off the core concepts of Ethics, Rights, and Accountability.

What is personal accountability?

Personal Accountability is a willingness to honestly answer for the results of our choices.

Let's get into it.

#BeAccountable

It's the Principalities (for me)…

Accountability Principles

Careful Attention.
Intentionality.
Compassion.
Truthfulness.
Resolve.

In principle number one, THINK BEFORE YOU ACT.

Learning to choose carefully what we want to do because our actions carry results.

In principle number two, BE INTENTIONAL

Makes a difference in how we SHOW UP. Not only for ourselves but especially for others.

Principle number three reminds us to HAVE COMPASSION.

Remaining mindful of the energy we put out, understanding that this is causing the results we are seeing/experiencing.

In principle four, ADMIT TO YOUR mistakes.

One of the main principles that sounds easier said than done also requires the most self-work.

Admit to it but don't stay in it. It's ok to heal.

The fifth and final principle is RESOLVE.

Learning from your own mistakes to avoid repeating them.

Principalities will get you cut off more than the hurt will.

Give thanks, and remain humble.

Expect nothing, and appreciate everything.

Choose humility.

REMAIN CONSISTENT

"I do worship you."
- John P. Kee

Staying humble and being humble will often remind you how separate each act of grace really is. It is generally easier for us to praise and worship, thank the Most High, walk around happy, and, for the most part, be pleased when we *feel like* things are going well and going our way. But what happens when life gets disrupted?

Proverbs 11:2 reminds us, "When pride comes, then comes disgrace, but with the humble is wisdom." Humility brings wisdom, while pride brings embarrassment. As humans, we are deeply flawed in our obsession with pride. This means we allow ourselves the option of comparison. We tend to show behaviors of fitting in, and we often forget that showing up exactly as who we are is not what is needed but has become what is required in spaces of intentional familiarity. It shows up everywhere, almost even daily. At some point in our learning and growing through life, some of us were even taught that pride was noble if it brought forth respect and honor among our peers, not knowing that anyone with this mindset would, at some point, be deceived. In the Proverbs reading, we learn that no matter the reason we allow pride to come in, it comes with shame because shame is permanently linked to pride. Humble yourself and give thanks.

Pride carries a load full of heavy consequences. Allowing yourself to take full accountability for your own healing is a start and requires discipline. *44 Days of Being Humble* stresses finding and creating your *own* disciplines and/or practices to maintain a healthy, *disciplined lifestyle*, so when things randomly get tough, you can choose humility over pride. When you're not in positions where you have a point to be made, you choose humility over pride. Even when you are on the brink of making hard decisions, choosing humility over pride becomes organic. Staying humble requires this. Being able to add a new level of discernment as we recognize and acknowledge that "Every day is new."

Discipline is truly the key to our very own strength. Find peace in building strength and emotional well-being, for we do not know the plans He has for us. Be strong enough to carry any load that will help with your internal and emotional building process. *Faith without work is truly dead. Put in work.*

Stay Humble.

Give thanks.

Cycles

"Didn't I conquer this last year?"
- Jonathan McReynolds

You're either going to repeat the cycle or evolve.

When a holy discontent or an annoying agitation surfaces, we are in an uncomfortable place of growth. God understands the importance of exits.

We don't.

Proverbs 16:3 reminds us to commit to the Lord whatever you do, and He will establish our plans. During life, we, at some point, realize that we don't know our very own plans. We have no clue what or where our true place of destiny lies. We fall into routines where we wake up, attend to hygiene/personal care, prepare for the day, and participate in the day. Most of the focus of participation is in our careers, where we commit to patterns of having tasks or daily assignments completed. Then we hit a season where we find ourselves en route to someone else's destiny with little to no consideration of our very own. We lose sight. Not that we aren't supposed to lose sight because if there is no purpose, there is no plan. When you're on someone else's journey, every twist and every turn feels wrong. It feels like you sink deeper and deeper into a place you are not familiar with, and it seems difficult to maneuver throughout.

The allowance of having your steps ordered is an intentional plea to let God have His way, for "He knows the plans He has for you." In fact, Jeremiah 29:11, reminds us of this. This message is from the Lord. "I have good plans for you. I don't plan to hurt you. I plan to give you hope and a good future."

Given this, why would we not follow His direction? Once realizing there's no such thing as a life that's greater than your own, this needed affirmation will have you determined to reach the other side of any mountain that you will face.

Our destiny is God's purpose for our lives. It is our God-ordained future. Destiny is what God has destined us to become in His divine will and wisdom. All in all, if God is for us, who truly can be against us?

Stay humble.

Taking a hard look at the quality and patterns of your friendships with others will give you a better understanding of who is a friend worth keeping. Are you a friend worth keeping? Is it time for your journeys to separate, to allow one's growth? Consider to what degree each person's values align with the direction of you reaching your own destination.

Your journey is your own.

Lovely Days

*"When I wake up in the morning love
and my heart is filled with pain"*
- Kirk Franklin

This is a day that we have never seen before! For that reason alone, I AM HUMBLE. Grateful to say the least.

"Every day is New" has become one of my favorite daily affirmations. Not only are these facts, but the day you are facing is indeed not a day that you have ever seen before. Therefore, it is new. The appreciation that I have found in the opportunity to see that newness of each day is beyond rewarding, in knowing that our expiration on this Earth remains the will of God. I am humbled by this. God is great.

Of course, we need to run, not walk, to the New King James Version for this affirmation. Proverbs 118:24 humbly reminds us that this is the day the Lord has made. We will rejoice and be glad in it.

Being joyful requires work. Most people don't just wake up happy or joyful if they are facing day-to-day issues. We all must put in work. Joy is rooted in who God is. It is not fleeting or based on circumstances that we are facing. Worldly possessions, accomplishments, and even the people in our lives are blessings that make us happy and fuel our personal joyfulness. Each day we face, we should challenge ourselves more and more to allow gratitude to lead our day, each day. We should be able to wake up giving thanks for the new day, the newness of it, and everything new within it. In doing this, we also give ourselves grace once we get through it. We are too hard on ourselves.

I read a church's signage as I was driving one day that said, "With joy comes clarity; with clarity comes comprehension." I loved this. Being in a place of clarity while transitioning through seasons of discernment will save you. This, too, will guide us in the direction of our very own destiny, as opposed to fitting into one's predetermined journey. "Your journey is your own."

Finding joy during trials will be one of the hardest things you will need to do. Discipline will be required. There's no way around it. First, we need to understand that the joy the world gives is not the same as the joy the Spirit gives. The Spirit's joy or happiness can stay with you for the long haul. On the other hand, the world will fold.

For the believer, the fruit of the Spirit, including joy, is like a bottomless well of water—there's always an abundant supply. Even in the darkest days, when sadness, grief, and loss may threaten to overwhelm you, God's joy is there.

Be Humble.

Be Joyful.

Intentional

"All things are working for my good,
He's intentional, never failing."
- Travis Greene

Consciousness and Intentionality.

Being conscious is defined as the state of being awake and aware of one's surroundings. The fact of awareness by the mind of itself and the world. When studying the concepts of consciousness, I've learned there were five levels to this understanding. For me to fully understand a new level of awareness, or to embrace a full-level mindset, I had to dig deep. Futures consciousness consists of five dimensions: time perspective, agency beliefs, openness to alternatives, systems perception, and concern for others.

Time Perspective: thinking and lack of consideration of consequences are the result of a limited time perspective.

Agency Beliefs: Fatalism, a passive attitude towards the future or a lack of responsibility for one's own actions may result from limited agency beliefs.

Openness to Alternatives: The opposite includes being uncritically optimistic or pessimistic, accepting authority without questioning, or an over reliance on past experiences to understand the future.

System Perception: Being unable to see ourselves as part of these various systems leads to suboptimal solutions or makes us incapable of understanding our responsibilities because of disconnection.

Concern for Others: A failure to develop this dimension may reduce an individual's understanding of the importance of the common good and may lead to a self-centered lifestyle or lack of deeper meaning in life.

Futures consciousness is the human capacity to understand, anticipate, prepare for, and embrace the future.

Proverbs 24:27 reminds us to prepare your work outside.

Get everything ready for yourself in the field, and after that, build your house.

#mindfulness

Pray for your Friends

"Every Praise is to our God"
-Bishop Hezekiah Walker

I am unable to truly forget all the good He continues to do for me. A lot of times, I am in true disbelief that God chooses to cover me the way He does. Why am I so deserving of this? Why are any of us?

Proverbs 17:17 teaches us to pray for our friendships.

Why is this important? How do we pray for our friendships properly as we navigate the journey of life for ourselves? In asking, "Lord, help us to love people around us in a way that blesses them in every circumstance." They walk especially through hard times, in the middle of adversity. We trust that we were born, at least in part, to help others walk through different kinds of adversity. When do you stop to ask, how well are you showing up for friends?

In the practice of being humble, a certain level of disconnection seems required in this space. You first must learn how to properly title those of important history, in which we make our friends along the way. Never to discredit the goodness of the memories your old friends bring. Everyone will not remain for you, or you for them, and that's ok. If God is for you, who shall be against you? These are new chapters that require new roles of friendship. As we grow, our circles are filled with those like-minded in thinking, equally yoked in decision-making, and those rooted in building empires of new growth.

It is easier said than received.

In the practice of staying humble, we recognize the absence of being present is more of an excuse versus the intentionality of being distant. Learning how to truly set proper boundaries versus putting up walls was hard for me. But once you figure it out, boundaries are non-negotiables. In some parts of our lives, we will notice the efforts we contribute to the existence of anything versus not being able to recognize when we have done too much. Put forth all the efforts you had. This will drain you. In most cases, people will do one of two things (the same goes for how you are contributing to their life). We are either adding inspiration to the room, or we are draining the energy that's left from it.

Inspire the room.

Favor Still Isn't Fair

"Love is patience, caring, love is kind.
Love is felt most when it's genuine."
- Bishop Hezekiah Walker

Proverbs 14:30 reminds us that a heart at peace gives life to the body, but envy rots the bones. In this word, there will be hate we know this all too well. The devil is mentioned as coming to steal, kill, and/or destroy. His plans are undated in doing this.

No matter how much love you have ever received up to this point, wherever you are in your current journey of life, stay humble…stay true. As you grow through life, learning to speak the life that you want over your entire being will become a priority in your daily lifestyle the more you are in your very own purpose. Speaking life and prosperity into yourself will become a mandate for the joy you fulfill in your own life. Whatever you encounter in your trials, your tests, and hard times, God releases abundant favor. In studies, we learn that in science, the spreading of joy is part of what is called "the macronutrients of happiness." This is from the study of the 4 Pillars of Happiness: to be grateful, to prioritize friends and family, to do and experience more, and to help others. I love this theory. The idea is to be intentional in spreading joy.

Gaining mindfulness seemed appropriate with life's new teachings. Yes, it was clear that we can never dictate or determine the actions of others.

In this response, we should have more of a drive to focus on the response that we bring to the table. Learning how to respond will be key to maintaining discipline. Or should I say taking full accountability for our response once the infliction has been made? Ask for clarity. Clarity to see with your eyes open!

Each day, your mind will try to wander on its own, controlling how you think, feel, and act. But by being mindful, we can train ourselves to live in the present moment to handle obstacles with a clear mind to help us live our best lives.

Each day, the enemy is fighting for your clarity. When he can't get you to self-destruct, in the moment of his presence, he will allow barriers of confusion to distract you from your purpose. If you're distracted from your purpose, operating freely in this world becomes one of human nature where you're likely to conform to the World.

Remain humble.

Give thanks.

Your Love

"It goes beyond all knowledge, your love"
- Fred Hammond

Seeking Mindfulness, Gaining Clarity.

When something on the inside starts working from the outside, what a blessing. We don't always know what this feeling is but we trust the process.

Being a person who wants to understand everything, then hearing that "God can give you the peace that passes *all* understanding...

Yes, you have my attention.

Proverbs 16:7 reminds us that when people make good choices, He is pleased; He even causes their enemies to live peacefully near them. Philippians 4:6-7 goes on to say not to be anxious about anything, but in everything by prayer and supplication with thanksgiving let your requests be made known to God. And the peace of God, which surpasses all understanding, will guard your hearts and your minds in Christ Jesus.

The peace that surpasses understanding is a supernatural peace that God offers us during our trials. It is a peace that defies explanation and human logic.

When we bring in human logic, we are entertaining thoughts of self-discovery, self-awareness, and even self-evaluation. What is truly disturbing your peace? The result of not knowing how to properly channel your emotional energy can lead to spaces of desperation, uncomforted, and usually feelings of anxiety and stress. Left unacknowledged, this can spiral into uncontrolled emotions. Never let your emotions outweigh your purpose or even your common sense. Achieving your inner peace in today's world is something that many strive for, but few achieve. **44 Days of Being Humble** reminded some and introduced to most a personal practice of discipline. Challenge yourself to work hard on keeping what you've strived so hard to achieve.

> *"He will turn your mourning into dancing."*

He Turned It.

"The devil though he had me, he thought my life was over."
-Tye Tribbett

It's not over until God says it's over. Be glad about that.

Often situations we've faced are confirmation enough that we should not still be here, operating freely on this Earth. Our own bad decisions should have taken us out. If it had not been for God on our sides, where would we be?

Proverbs 24:16 assures us, for a just man falls seven times and rises again, but the wicked will fall into mischief.

A peace that passes understanding.

What we lack to understand is that God, too, has the choice to cover and protect his children. What if our lives are solely dependent on our actions and repercussions? The path to inner peace is not a one-size-fits-all approach. You may choose not to embark on the spiritual route at all, and instead, try to do everything perfectly according to society's standards. In doing this, we get weak, we get tired. All because this requires work. Faith without work is truly dead. Having an active faith following the art of maintaining a daily discipline can change your entire life.

What's life without peace?

Inner peace is always with us. The problem is that inner peace gets disturbed when we interact *with* the world, and especially when acting *of* the world. As humans, we form opinions and commentary about the things that happen to us. When we are still and quiet and can observe instead of commentating on everything, we are able to achieve inner peace, and inner thought processing.

Taking full accountability for how you contribute to your own peace being interrupted will be top tier in your personal journey. The art of accountability is generally defined within four steps.

See it, own it, solve it, and DO IT!

Stay Humble.

The 5 Levels of Obedience

In this crazy life, we must remind ourselves, that achieving a culture of accountability starts with aligning your own results with your own actions. This might seem like common sense, but unfortunately, it's not such a common practice. Everything we go through is a stepping stool or preparation where God is attempting to take us. In His will, not yours.

God is Faithful.

Proverbs 1:2 reminds us to know wisdom and instruction; To discern the words of understanding.

Being obedient to the instructions of God's promise is a path for purpose. "God blesses those who obey him" (Proverbs 16:20 TLB). Let it be His will, never yours. Having wisdom in times of destruction can bring you back or lead you to a place of peace. Allowing you the space to discern. With wisdom, comes truth.

In psychology, there are two forms of obedience defined—constructive obedience and destructive obedience. The former involves an order that is positive to society, such as a person following traffic safety laws. The latter entails an order that is negative to society, such as a soldier shooting unarmed civilians.

Tools are essential throughout our studying and learning. Justin G. Gravitt provides a framework titled The 5 Levels of Obedience.

Level 1: *Inconsistent Obedience* - Doing what you want

Level 2: *Conditional Obedience* - An Exchange of (Agape) Love

Level 3: *Provisional Obedience* - "As long as" (Expectational Faith)

Level 4: *Future-Happiness Obedience* - (at some point) type of Faith

Level 5: *Unconditional Obedience* - Giving Him what He wants

> *"I know, O Lord, that a man's life is not his own; it is not for man to direct his steps."*
>
> – Jeremiah 10:23

Assessing your Obedience Levels is great practice for adding to your daily discipline practices/performances. (discipleship.org/blog/5-levels-of-obedience-tool/)

Conspiracy Isn't the Theory

"They whispered, conspired, they told their lies.
God favors me."
- Bishop Hezekiah Walker

Having favor from God must be one of the largest gifts He can offer you. This is a gift that the Lord provides without expectation or in exchange for anything, not even good work.

Proverbs 8:33-35 reminds us to listen to His teaching and be wise; don't ignore what He says. Whoever waits at His door and listens for Him will be blessed. Those who find Him find life, and the Lord will reward them.

Merriam-Webster defines a person having grace to be one with "a controlled, polite, and pleasant way of behaving." To the world, it is a way of carrying oneself. It is seen as a trait that plays out through actions. As we grow through life, we understand how massive our behavior will contribute to the produce of life's harvest. You will reap what you sow.

Remain mindful. Mindfulness during healing will allow a clear(er) space for thinking. For discernment to do the expected task in separating how we feel versus what we know. May the favor of God be with us as we figure ourselves out. Being accountable in your seasons of healing will often too, remind us that God's grace is sufficient. Your measure of faith will be tested in knowing that all you need and deserve is Him. The opposite of grace is the desire to get back at someone for what they have done to you, to "make them pay." It is not just getting what someone deserves (which is justice), but the desire to make another person own your pain by inflicting pain upon them in some way. Some would call this vengeance.

Romans 12:19-21 states: Beloved, never avenge yourselves, but leave it to the wrath of God, for it is written, "Vengeance is mine, I will repay, says the Lord."

To the contrary, "If your enemy is hungry, feed him; if he is thirsty, give him something to drink; for by so doing, you will heap burning coals on his head." Do not be overcome by evil but overcome evil with good.

When we take vengeance on others, we do it out of hatred, wrath, malice, judgmentalism, arrogance, enmity, spite, unkindness, and other sinful motives. In other words, vengeance is not righteous.

God Will.

Pure Joy

"God has smiled on me."
- Jessica Reedy

Proverbs 15:13-18 reminds us, If you are happy, your face shows it. If you are sad, your spirit feels defeated. Intelligent people want more knowledge, but fools only want more nonsense. Life is always hard for the poor, but the right attitude can turn it into a party. It is better to be poor and respect the Lord than to be rich and have many troubles. It is better to eat a little where there is love than to eat a lot where there is hate. A quick temper causes fights, but patience brings peace and calm. That was deep.

Arthur Rubinstein says, "Do not let your spirit get defeated. A defeated heart is a stoned heart, and a stoned heart is one past the limitations of being hurt, wounded, or inflicted. Do not be dismayed. Life is the game that must be played, this truth at least, good friends, we know; so live and laugh, nor be dismayed as one by one the phantoms go."

Happiness is about being able to make the most of the good times but also, to cope effectively with the inevitable bad times. Or, in the words of the biochemist turned Buddhist monk Matthieu Ricard, "Happiness is a deep sense of flourishing, not a mere pleasurable feeling or fleeting emotion but an optimal state of being."

Learn to control your emotions. Learn that only you will be able to determine your day-to-day happiness. Once you realize that you are truly the writer, producer, and actor of your own screenplay, life will become more enjoyable. By nature, we begin giving ourselves permission where there were previously barriers. We allow ourselves to trust ourselves more. How beautiful is this? Joy is like food for the soul. Which is imperative to our mind, body, and soul healing journey. If you find yourself stuck in despair, try obeying the Bible's instruction to love God and others. When we obey His commandment to love one another, we are striving to live according to His word.

> *"I have found that if you love life, life will love you back."*
> – Arthur Rubinstein

Who Are We to Judge?

"He without sin, cast the first stone."
- Le'Andria Johnson

Only those who are faultless have the right to pass judgment on others (implying that no one is faultless and that, therefore, no one has such a right to pass judgment). This is the meaning of one "casting the first stone."

Proverbs 25:8-11 (Easy-to-Read) reminds us not to be too quick to tell a judge about something you saw. You will be embarrassed if someone else proves you wrong. If you want to tell your friends about your own problems, tell them. But don't discuss what someone told you in private. Whoever hears it will lose their respect for you and will never trust you again. Saying the right thing at the right time is like a golden apple in a silver setting.

When writing this, I struggled with which translation of the reading would best support and clarify the scripture. The easy-to-read version listed tells us, straight to the point with no additional Greek methodology to not judge a soul. Who are we REALLY to judge? Though we have heard the same or similar colloquialisms to remind us how frowned upon judgment can be or even result in, we do this so naturally. The Art of Judgement explores how judgments are formed. In focus, the inherently dynamic nature of both assessments and decisions, as they are produced, validated, and redefined through constant processes of mediation and conflict, both synchronically and diachronically. Learning, through your heart, that because we are not designed the same, our differences and opinions will come. Let us not be so quick to blame, criticize, or even punish. Who are we to judge our peers? The tables will soon turn.

#remainhumble

Staying Humble (Grounded)
The Importance of Chakra Health and Spiritual Wellness

Chakra health is essential to maintaining overall physical, emotional, and spiritual well-being. When the chakras are in balance, energy flows freely through the body, promoting good health and vitality. However, when there are blockages or imbalances in the chakras, it can lead to physical and emotional symptoms such as pain, tension, anxiety, and depression. Chakra healing techniques, such as meditation and yoga, have been found to be effective in relieving these symptoms and promoting overall health and well-being.

In *44 Days of Being Humble*, we highlighted the importance of mental detoxing and creating discipline. In addition to mental healing, physical healing is imperative. The focus we took on the importance of the Root Chakra (Muladhara) is responsible for our sense of security, stability, and safety. Our focus in *44 Days of Staying Humble* was about aligning with sexual and creative energy and linking to how you relate to and connect with others. This will forever be important in how we are operating in life. Areas of aligning our sexual energy and/or creative energy are harder to align than most other chakra healing. Driven in inspiration, this can be a blockage to your growth if the wrong or too much energy is allowed.

Have boundaries, be selective, remain creative. Remain focused.

In Essence, we will always recognize when our energies are not aligned with our purpose. The war within will be a personal battle. Never stop recognizing your triggers, always allow room for growth, and be prepared to feel the attack within. Hard lessons are the epitome of reaching the peak of your destiny. Your faith is increased in knowing that if He can do it for them, He can do it for you. Remove pride boundaries, align your energy, and adjust your soul. This is not always an easy practice. Incorporating fasting and/or detox practices will release bodily toxins.

What can we supplement to align and adjust our mental? More peace.

Give thanks (for it all).

It's ok to heal.

Long Humble Faith

"Who opens doors, that I cannot see? Jesus will."
-Anita Wilson

There are things in this life that are just waiting for our arrival. It's already yours, it's waiting for you. Having strong faith will be one thing. Having *long* faith, will keep you blessed.

Proverbs 2:8-9 reminds us, "He guards the paths of the just and protects those who are faithful to him." Then you will understand what is right and just and fair—every good path.

In life, we were usually reminded to stay anchored in faith. To lean not on our own understanding when gaining order in our lives. How can we not lean? God reminds us often, that He will not build where things can be compromised. God is a God of order. If He feels like it is for you, it no doubt will be right there waiting for you. Avoid becoming so empty in the unraveling process that you forget that there is nothing too big for Him. There is purpose in His entire plan for you. Stay Humble.

Sustaining faith in the long term can be the most challenging thing to do, for we are never prepared to have what we would consider enough faith when things go wrong or get tough. It's been studied to confirm that the main shift in the faith perspective between now and twenty years ago is towards what they described as a more open, and less narrow form of faith. This shift was particularly clear in those who no longer go to church, but it was also a clear direction for those who are still attending church. It doesn't discredit the fact that the world needs a liberating and life-changing kind of love. The core task of the church is to show how this pursuit can be met through faith in Jesus. In a complex world, the church is community.

Have faith, never stop.

CHOICES

"Eyes haven't seen, Ears haven't heard,
All you have planned for me."
- Brian Courtney Wilson

"God forgives. I don't."
- Rick Ross

When God meets you in your despair, it is a humble reminder of how immeasurable his grace and favor can be. There is truly nothing on this beautiful green Earth to separate Him from you. With God enveloping us in love and strength, we have absolutely no reason to fear the future or life after death.

Proverbs 31:25 reminds us, Strength and honor are her clothing; she is confident about the future.

When you believe that you are worth fighting for, you will be worth fighting for. What is the measure of your worth? How do you truly see yourself? Shame and fear can be misunderstood as the "fear of connection." What makes you feel less than? Allowing yourself to be seen, in real-time, allows one to deconstruct shame. This leads to vulnerability.

In life, Ego seems more important to satisfy than self-development. The unlearning of how to put away prideful ways in any situation where it stood forefront takes daily work. A case study by Paul Tripp confirms, "You cannot read the Proverbs without concluding that your body only goes where your heart has already gone; your mouth only goes where your heart has already gone; your eyes only go where your heart has already gone." The range of the different heart types helps us to understand that the heart is the epitome of control over your mind and your body, leading to your soul. Meaning, whatever has your heart has domination of your center being. This is what drives each of us to move towards a purpose.

In purpose, too, learning how to forgive properly will be essential to the measure of growth in your next level. Forgiveness is first. It is the reminder of how we are "in this world but not of this world." We were not all raised the same. Being raised off love versus being bought up on survival, becomes uncomfortably unfitting when you were raised to meet the world where they were. A combination of both, or some would say, "being book smart and streets smart." Being green is for the birds. Develop ways to forgive versus retaliate. Thank God for His forever grace and kind mercy.

Being humble is a choice.

Unbroken

"There is Power in the Name of Jesus"
- Tasha Cobb Leonard

With God's help, your steps will be ordered, your words will be sweet, and your thoughts completely pure, following with only the purist intentions. There will still be areas in our lives where we may feel stuck, unmotivated, or unmoved. We must break those chains.

There's a trick to the graceful exit.

It begins with the vision to recognize when a job, a life stage, a relationship is over and to let it go. In the words of Ellen Goodman, "It means leaving what's over without denying its value."

Steve Maraboli once quoted, "The truth is, unless you let go, unless you forgive yourself, unless you forgive the situation, unless you realize that the situation is over, you cannot move forward."

Proverbs 17:9 translates that, "one who seeks love conceals an offense, but one who repeats it divides friends."

Discontent is a hellish sin because, at its heart, it is an expression of rebellion against God. Our responses are not always pleasing to the Most High. We must learn to forgive fully—wholeheartedly.

Forgiveness is powerful. Learning how to forgive becomes difficult when it's not easy to forget the offense. With intention, realize and admit your part in any situation/conflict. Ask the ultimate forgiver, the Most High, to empower you, remembering that He, too, has forgiven His beautiful children. Decide that you don't want to keep on letting that person(s) or situation hurt you by holding the grudge and hurting others along the way. I know it is easier said than done as most of us want our "lick back." But that is not where our focus should be. Focus on God. Have faith that although the moment does not feel good, it is preparation for the next level of growth that He has in store for you. There is nothing too big for God.

Often, I would have to remind myself, "If God is for me, who can be against me." I heard in response to this, the devil. The fallen angel is still in the business of stealing, killing, and destroying. God's will is forever greater than yours.

May the Lord provide peace that passes all of your understanding.

Be Still.

Be Humble.

Wise Counsel

"What do you do,
when you've done all that you can?
Just Stand."

- Donnie McClurkin

Doing nothing may seem weighted to most. Akin to wasting time and depleting inspiration. This is not really the preferred first thought or ideal of "figuring it out," but we all have been there.

Proverbs 1:1-2 is there to remind us that we are all just trying to figure things out. These are the proverbs of Solomon, the son of David and king of Israel. They will help you learn to be wise, to accept correction, and to understand wise sayings. This feels like an amazing reassurance that if we seek, we will find.

The entire purpose of the book of Proverbs, I would like to think, is to become like the wise or even wiser. To learn how to walk with them, then to learn how to gain your own mental understanding of their humble teachings.

"Sometimes, if not most of the time, you find out who you are by figuring out who and what you are not." – Author, Kelly Cutrone.

Learning how to unlearn, re-construct, detach and sometimes reattach in seasons where we are moving in a forward motion can seem off. There will be moments of shame because we cannot figure things out in the way we thought we could, in the timing we had planned in our own minds or even second-guessing the original reason that we bring ourselves into a moment. This is never about the feelings. It is all about the desire, to learn to seek God. To truly seek Him to a level of knowing that He is ever-present. Learn to quiet your soul. Investing your most into the cost of paying attention.

In those quiet seasons, never forget to purge.

This is in reference to the purification or cleansing process.

This means to let go. Get rid of things that are no longer serving you—mentally, spiritually, and emotionally. In purging, you are usually re-introduced or introduced to the version of you that you lost, never got to, or simply forgot that you had because, along the way, this version of you was reduced to serving others. The relief is worth the exchange.

Stay Humble.

Just Breathe (Unplug)

Learning to "Sit with Yourself"

It is already done. The plans are already made, the provisions have been set forth. Learn to allow your soul to rest. In the season of waiting, rest.

Proverbs 23:9-35 reminds us, "Don't try to teach fools. They will make fun of your wise words. Never move an old property line, and don't take land that belongs to orphans. The Lord will be against you. He is powerful and protects orphans. Listen to your teacher and learn all you can. Always correct children when they need it. If you spank them, it will not kill them. In fact, you might save their lives. My son, it makes me happy when you make a wise decision. It makes me feel good inside when you say the right things. Never envy evil people, but always respect the Lord. This will give you something to hope for that will not disappoint you. So listen, my son, and be wise. Always be careful to follow the right path. Don't make friends with people who drink too much wine and eat too much food. Those who eat and drink too much become poor. They sleep too much and end up wearing rags. Listen to your father. Without him, you would never have been born. Respect your mother, even when she is old. Truth, wisdom, learning, and understanding are worth paying money for. They are worth far too much to ever sell. The father of a good person is very happy. A wise child brings him joy. Make both of your parents happy. Give your mother that same joy. My son, listen closely to what I am saying. Let my life be your example. Prostitutes and bad women are a trap. They are like a deep well that you cannot escape. A bad woman waits for you like a thief, and she causes many men to be unfaithful to their wives. Who gets into fights and arguments? Who gets hurt for no reason and has red, bloodshot eyes? People who stay out too late drinking wine, staring into their strong drinks. So be careful with wine. It is pretty and red as it sparkles in the cup. And it goes down so smoothly when you drink it. But in the end, it will bite like a snake. Wine will cause you to see strange things and to say things that make no sense. When you lie down, you will think you are on a rough sea and feel like you are at the top of the mast. You will say, 'They hit me, but I never felt it. They beat me, but I don't remember it. Now I can't wake up. I need another drink.'"

This whole page was confirmation from the Most High. He never stops pursuing us.

#Godisamazing

Just breathe.

Sacral Chakra (Shadow Work)

"The Sanskrit name [for the sacral chakra] is Svadhisthana," says certified chakra and crystal healer Laura Konst. "The symbol of the sacral chakra is a moon crescent, which represents the relationship between the tides of water and the phases of the moon."

Shadow issues, or negative qualities, associated with the sacral chakra include:
- *wounded emotions*
- *secrets*
- *fear of judgment, getting into trouble, or being "found out"*
- *repression*
- *inability to experience emotional or sexual intimacy*
- *nightmares and not remembering or understanding dreams*

According to previous studies, signs of an overactive sacral chakra can include:
- *feeling consumed by your emotions, as if drowning in them*
- *experiencing emotional ups and downs*
- *using escapism to avoid life*
- *showing obsessive affection that isn't returned*
- *engaging in inappropriate expressions of sexuality*

"You may try to retain a sense of control by lashing out and exhibiting controlling and manipulating behaviors toward others," she says. "Imbalances can manifest in both spectrums and lead to emotional outbursts or an apathetic and disconnected attitude."

**Candice Covington, author of "Essential Oils in Spiritual Practice"

Breaking the Cycles Within

"Break every Chain"
-Tasha Cobb Leonard

Cycles occur when cycles are the only thing we know.

For us to transition to the next level, there are likely things we must too, leave behind. Things that, by choice or even haphazardly, will pick up.

In growing, we are like flowers. Our souls are rooted in the soil of our upbringing. We are watered by the people in our lives and the people we encounter. We stem, have pricks, blossom, and transition into beautiful new things.

Proverbs 23:18 reminds us, "For sure there is a future and your hope will not be cut off." Blessed assurance.

Transitioning through life is a beautiful journey. We are moved from one level of innocence to another, the beauty of life connecting to our unforeseen future. While on the journey, we realize, in those moments, if we are the person who appreciates the journey in order to reach destiny. Or are we the person whose goal is just to reach destiny, by any means? This is important to recognize so that there are never fears of "getting it wrong versus right." Being able to properly place standards on oneself, takes a lot of effort. Just as much effort as we put into trying to prove to someone else what we can bring to the table. This is the integrity mentioned in *44 Days of Being Humble.* Your journey is your own.

This is a humble reminder that there is a very thin line between showing up when able and people-pleasing. Having a fair understanding of how to be there for and with yourself will have you in complete alignment with everything for you, with you, and destined for you. Remain humble. It always gets better.

But God.

Winning Season

"You Will Win"
- Jekalyn Carr

Shout out to everything and everyone who wanted you to lose.

You will win.

Having this degree of confidence is literal music to anyone's ears who is in their "winning season." It is also music to the ones no longer rooting for you. A different genre, but they "hear" you, and they see you. Keep winning.

Proverbs 11:30 humbly reminds us that the fruit of those who are right with God is a tree of life, and he who wins souls is wise.

Be wise. Remain humble. Remain selective.

Everything attached to you will win, is able to win, and cannot afford to lose in one more season. You are here because you chose discipline over distraction. In *44 Days of Being Humble*, the goal is to maintain and develop your own winning strategy, because of consistent faith, humility, and discipline.

Stay Humble.

This will require the same level of faith, added discipline, and focus to maintain clarity. If you want it, you will have it.

Train your mind to be focused to win in any emotional state. Emotional imbalance can be the downfall to your winning if you allow it. The clearer your mind, the better your decisions will be. Discern in every season.

Remember, too, that in all or most situations regarding winning, someone must lose. Losing doesn't have to be negative or anything frowned upon. Losing humbly can be the translation of what needs to be done better the next time. It is the lesson in which we teach ourselves what worked and did not work in the areas of needed growth. We can take accountability in taking a loss. This gives us strength, in most cases, a strength that we would have never known we needed, had we not taken the loss. God is able. God is still good.

Win regardless.

Transformative Transactions

"Amazing Grace, how sweet the sound"
- CeCe Winans

There are times when we will have the willingness—the humility—to allow ourselves to be disrupted by others. We show up for them. We put others first. Overall, we have more integrity for others that we do for ourselves. Humble yourself in doing this.

A heart renewal reveals everything that you are, and who you are called to be. Showing up for others is not the problem. However, being able to be present for or with others at the times that they need someone's presence is a blessing not always properly honored. It is an amazing, selfless act. Showing up for others when you are in positions of healing, grieving or recovery yourself to any degree is where we draw lines of integrity. Learning to show up for yourself will be the humility that you never knew you needed until YOU arrive. Stay humble.

Keep your heart pure, always. His ways are not your ways, and your thoughts are not His thoughts.

Be very glad about this.

Proverbs 22:11 reminds of that those who love a pure heart and speak with grace will find that the king is their friend. *What a friend we have in Jesus.* His Amazing grace is the sweetest sound. How many friendships do we have that "gift us" something new each day? Every day His mercies are new.

As we level through understanding ourselves, our ways, thoughts, and actions, we will be able to align our daily greatness with His greater purpose.

To know who you are and whose you are will save you from your own self.

To accept who others are, who others have become, and who others choose to be when you are in their presence, in the sake of integrity, service, and healing, may we continue to ask that they see God, not us.

Never forget that the cultivation of oneself is a continual shift into one's purpose.

In the weary state of the world, continue to seek hope. Never lose heart.

Harvest well. Water yourself. Humility will forever be key.

New Struggles
Create New Strength

*"May your struggles keep you near the cross.
May your troubles show that you need God."*

- Jonathan McReynolds

I felt this.

It is always healing to be reminded that your struggles create new strength. Surround me with humble reminders that Your grace will forever be sufficient.

Proverbs 31:25 states, "Clothed in strength and dignity, with nothing to fear, she smiles when she thinks about the future."

The importance of having a clear mindset, clearer than the previous season, will be a subconscious reminder of how to remain in your very own purpose versus the distractions and the misguidance of others. Take with you in every series, in every season, that there is a thin line between service and serving oneself. Your integrity for others speaks volumes to the integrity that you owe yourself. Let it forever be His will, never yours. Calm your mind, listen to your soul, and respect your purpose. Spend time with yourself to spend time with God.

Your future is what you make of it.

God is good. It *is* that simple.

Be humble. Stay humble.

Give thanks for it all.

The "Root" (Being Humble)

Having knowledge of the chakras system can be helpful for one's mental health. Rather than using each chakra as a basis for literal diagnosis, you can explore the meaning of each chakra and the ailments that present when it is unbalanced. This may support you in finding language for what you're experiencing. You will feel every change that your mind, body, and soul adjust to.

The wisdom gained from the book of Proverbs provides encouragement that "it is already done."

The dynamic of harmonizing good includes one's peace and others' blessings. Fear, worry, and doubt cannot exist in the same space as healing, peace, and wellness.

Detoxifying your mindset will help with transitioning to a place of conscious gratitude. Often we have unconscious thoughts that flow in through a sense of lack versus sensibility. Ask God to show you the next steps of your life and seek intentional purpose.

Intuition is real.

Not from lack but from fulfillment, completeness, humility, and gratitude.

When a person transitions to *their* purpose, their path becomes clear.

2 Weeks of Staying Humble

Iron sharpens Iron.

The wisdom gained from the book of Proverbs provides encouragement in knowing that *"it is already done."*

All practices mentioned are humbling opportunities for aligning one's mind, body, and soul while gaining spiritual and cultural wisdom. Doing the shadow work isn't easy, here you are, here is a challenge. Remembering that challenges require discipline. Disciple producing a renewal of growth. Every day is NEW. Give thanks.

Week One
Detox your MIND.

Day 1. Gain Insight: Proverbs 14:30 NIV

Day 2. Owning Discernment: Proverbs 16:21 NIV

Day 3. Guarding your Heart: Proverbs 4:23

Day 4. Seek Humility: Proverbs 23:17 NKJV

Day 5. Build Consistency: Proverbs 12:22 NRSV

Day 6. Gain Courage: Proverbs 13:17 NLT

Day 7. Focus on yourself: Proverbs 25:20 NLT

Week Two
Cleanse your SOUL.

Day 1. Gain Insight: Proverbs 14:30 NIV

Day 2. Owning Discernment: Proverbs 16:21 NIV

Day 3. Guarding your Heart: Proverbs 4:23

Day 4. Seek Humility: Proverbs 23:17 NKJV

Day 5. Build Consistency: Proverbs 12:22 NRSV

Day 6. Gain Courage: Proverbs 13:17 NLT

Day 7. Focus on yourself: Proverbs 25:20 NLT

The dynamic of harmonizing good includes one's peace and other's blessings. Fear, worry, or doubt cannot exist in the same space as healing, peace, and wellness.

Detoxifying your mind will help with transitioning to a place of conscious gratitude. Often, we have unconscious thoughts that allow ideas to flow in through a sense of lack versus sensibility. Ask God to show you the next steps of your life, and seek intentional purpose.

Intuition is real. Not from lack but from fulfillment, completeness, humility, and gratitude.

When a purpose transitions to their purpose, their path becomes clear.

Stay Humble. Give thanks for it all.